In loving memory of Karen Blumenthal,
a great writer and a great friend—M.S.

Dedicated to Stephanie and others who respect children's curiosity about life from
the darkest ocean abyss to the brightest distant stars—R.D.

We are grateful to Shannon Johnson, Senior Research Technician at Monterey Bay Aquarium Research
Institute in Moss Landing, California, for sharing her time, expertise, and enthusiasm for the deep sea and
whale falls with us. Thank you for reviewing the book at various stages and answering at least 101 questions.

Text copyright © 2023 by Melissa Stewart • Jacket art and interior illustrations copyright © 2023 by Rob Dunlavey

All rights reserved. Published in the United States by Random House Studio, an imprint of Random House Children's
Books, a division of Penguin Random House LLC, New York.

Random House Studio and the colophon are registered trademarks of Penguin Random House LLC.

Visit us on the Web! rhcbooks.com
Educators and librarians, for a variety of teaching tools, visit us at RHTeachersLibrarians.com

Library of Congress Cataloging-in-Publication Data is available upon request.
ISBN 978-0-593-38060-4 (trade) — ISBN 978-0-593-38061-1 (lib. bdg.) — ISBN 978-0-593-38062-8 (ebook)

The artist used watercolor, mixed media, and digital tools to create the illustrations for this book.
The text of this book is set in 17-point Brandon Grotesque Medium.
Interior design by Rachael Cole

MANUFACTURED IN CHINA
10 9 8 7 6 5 4 3 2 1
First Edition

WHALE FALL

EXPLORING AN
OCEAN-FLOOR ECOSYSTEM

written by MELISSA STEWART
illustrated by ROB DUNLAVEY

RANDOM HOUSE STUDIO
NEW YORK

When a whale dies,
its massive body
silently sinks
down,
down,
through the inky darkness,
finally coming to rest
on the soft, silty seafloor.

For the whale, it's the end of a seventy-year life.

But for a little-known community of deep-sea denizens,
it's a new beginning. The whale fall is a bountiful gift that
can sustain life for another fifty years.

Hungry hagfish smell the whale from miles around and swarm the scene.

It may be their first meal in weeks.

Sleeper sharks smell the whale, too, but they
swim slowly through the frigid water.
When they arrive, they feast on skin and blubber.

Eventually, other scavengers arrive, too. Even after six months, roughscale rattails and snubnose eelpouts are still dining on bits of blubber, while grooved tanner crabs pick away at any leftovers they can find.

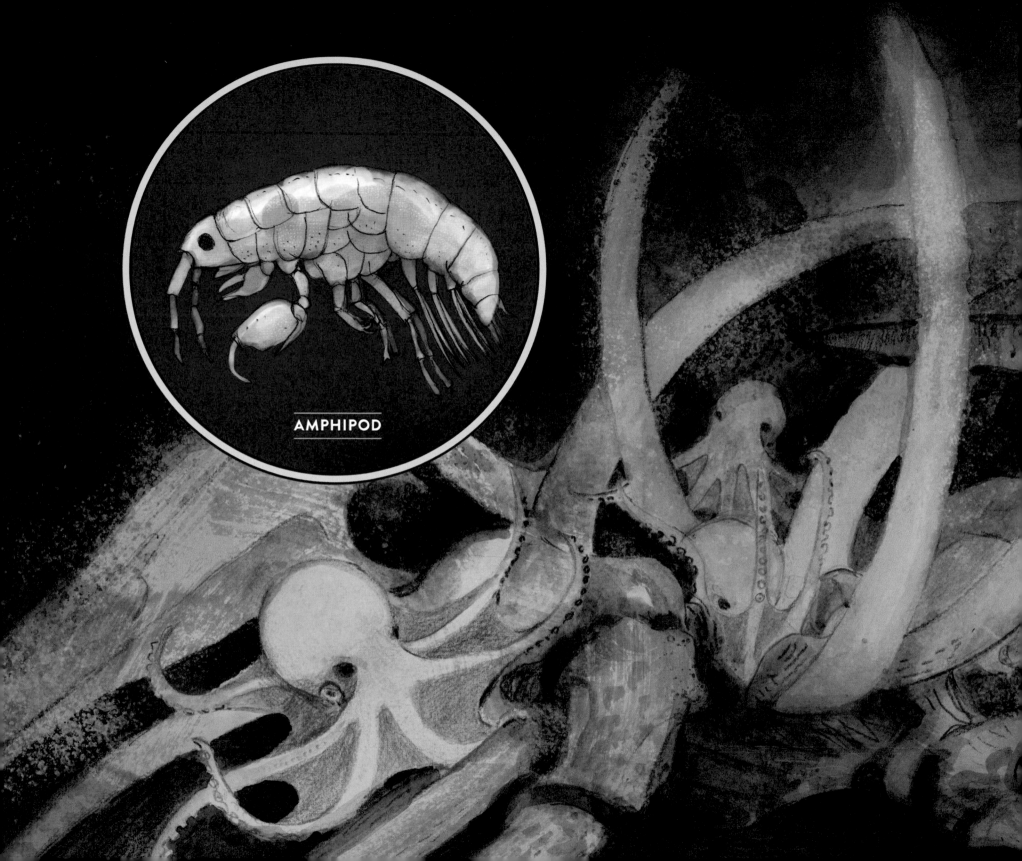

AMPHIPOD

Over the next year and a half, an army of tiny amphipods strips the whale's bones bare. As these mini-munchers feed, they attract the attention of hungry deep-sea octopuses.

HOODED SHRIMP

Meanwhile, Oregon hair crabs scarf up scraps that have fallen beneath the bones.

Tiny hooded shrimp and pink sea pigs sift through the sediment, hunting for tasty tidbits. These small scavengers make a hearty meal for a blob sculpin.

Even after the whale's bones are picked clean, the feast doesn't end. Clusters of zombie worms blanket the bones. As their frilly plumes wave through the water, their roots ooze acids that break down the bones. Then tiny Oceanospirillales bacteria living inside the worms' roots absorb fats and proteins that they—and the worms—need to survive.

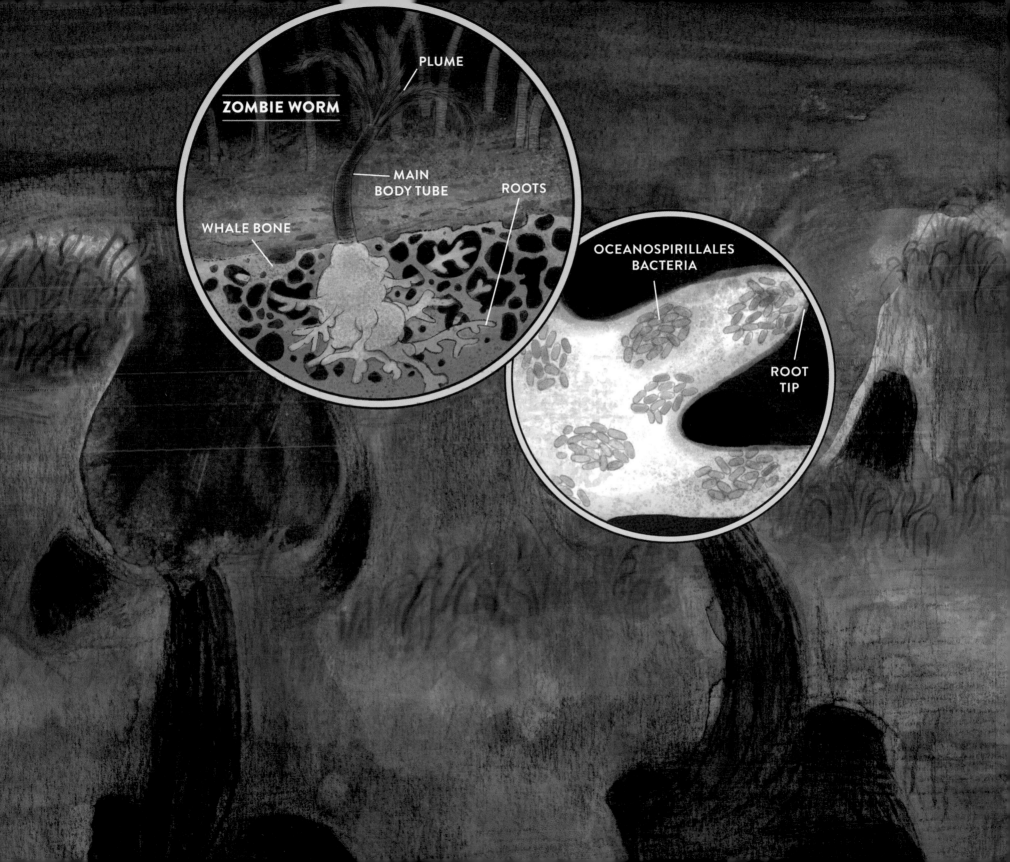

As squat lobsters dine on the zombie worms,
brittle stars search the seafloor for morsels of meat.
Sea cucumbers collect droplets of whale oil that
have soaked into the sediment.

After about two years, the zombie worms have trouble getting the nutrients they need to live and grow. As they die, bone-eating Deltaproteobacteria take their place.

Year after year, decade after decade, these tiny bone eaters tunnel through the whale skeleton. As they feed, they give off gases that many kinds of deep-sea microbes use to make food of their own.

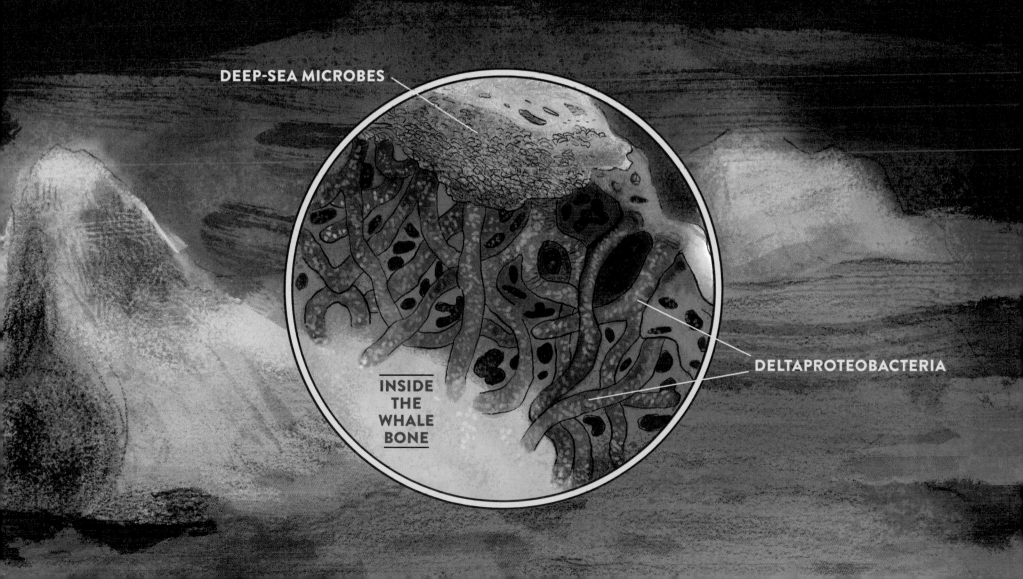

DEEP-SEA MICROBES

INSIDE
THE
WHALE
BONE

DELTAPROTEOBACTERIA

Some deep-sea microbes form thick, colorful mats that spread across the bones and cascade onto the seafloor.

While snails and limpets graze along the edges, scale worms chew trails right down the middle.

Other kinds of deep-sea microbes seek shelter inside mussels the size of a fingernail, clams the size of a fist, or clusters of tubeworms swaying in the current. To earn their keep, the tiny tenants make food for themselves and their host.

Eventually, every last trace of the mighty whale is gone.

But for fifty years, the whale fall was a thriving oasis that offered hundreds of species—millions of creatures—a much-needed source of food on the vast, barren seafloor.

And somewhere,

perhaps not so far away,

the cycle is beginning again.

MORE ABOUT WHALE FALLS

Each year, about 70,000 whales die of natural causes and sink to the seafloor. That might sound like a lot, but because the ocean is so huge, whale falls are usually spaced many miles apart.

The low temperatures and high pressure of the deep sea make it possible for large whales to slowly decompose over many decades, supporting a rich assortment of life. This book describes the creatures that might feed in, on, or around a 70,000-pound (32,000-kg) gray whale that has fallen to a depth of 5,000 feet (1,500 m) in the East Pacific Ocean. Whale falls at different depths or in other oceans will host a somewhat different cast of creatures.

Scientists had no idea that whale fall communities existed until 1987, when they discovered one off the coast of California. Since then, they've found about twenty-five more in oceans all over the world. By studying these sites (as well as dead whales they've sunk on purpose), researchers have identified more than 500 different species living on and around whale falls. Many of them are temporary visitors, but at least thirty species haven't been seen in any other environment.

MORE ABOUT SOME WHALE FALL SPECIES

As you read this section, notice how much we don't yet know about many of these animals. Exploring the deep sea poses all kinds of challenges, but scientists are learning more all the time about this incredible environment and the creatures living there. Maybe one day you'll do research that adds to our knowledge.

GRAY WHALE
Scientific name: *Eschrichtius robustus*
Size: Up to 49 feet (15 m) long
Diet: Amphipods, shrimp, worms, clams, crabs
Predators: Orcas
Life span: 50 to 70 years
Field note: Gray whales migrate 14,000 miles (22,000 km) a year.

BLACK HAGFISH
Scientific name: *Eptatretus deani*
Size: 25 inches (64 cm) long
Diet: Shrimp, worms, dead fish and whales
Predators: Sharks and other large fish
Life span: 40 years
Field note: Hagfish don't have bones or teeth. They grind food with tooth-like structures made of the same material as your fingernails.

PACIFIC SLEEPER SHARK

Scientific name: *Somniosus pacificus*
Size: 14 feet (4 m) long
Diet: Fish, seals, octopus, shrimp, crabs, dead whales
Predators: Orcas
Life span: Unknown
Field note: A Pacific sleeper shark is a real slowpoke. Its top speed is only 3 miles (5 km) per hour. A great white shark can swim ten times faster.

ROUGHSCALE RATTAIL

Scientific name: *Coryphaenoides acrolepis*
Size: 16 inches (41 cm) long
Diet: Anything that will fit in its mouth
Predators: Unknown
Life span: Up to 70 years
Field note: Rattails make a drumming sound to communicate with one another.

AMPHIPOD

Scientific name: Lysianassid family
Size: Less than 0.02 inch (0.05 cm) long
Diet: Dead animals
Predators: Gray whales, fish
Life span: About 1 year
Field note: Amphipods have fourteen legs. They use four to grab food and ten for swimming.

SNUBNOSE EELPOUT

Scientific name: *Pachycara bulbiceps*
Size: 20 inches (51 cm) long
Diet: Copepods, crabs, tubeworms, shrimp, dead whales
Predators: Unknown
Life span: Unknown
Field note: How did the eelpout get its name? It's shaped like an eel and looks like it's pouting.

GROOVED TANNER CRAB

Scientific name: *Chionoecetes tanneri*
Size: 2 to 3 inches (5 to 7 cm) wide
Diet: Brittle stars, worms, clams, mussels, dead whales
Predators: Seals, fish, octopuses, other crabs
Life span: Up to 20 years
Field note: When tanner crabs hatch from their eggs, they look more like shrimp than crabs.

HOODED SHRIMP

Scientific name: *Cumella*
Size: Up to 0.4 inch (1 cm) long
Diet: Dead material that has fallen to the seafloor
Predators: Fish
Life span: Unknown
Field note: About 1,000 species of hooded shrimp have been identified, but scientists think there are many more still to be discovered.

SEA PIG

Scientific name: *Scotoplanes globosa*
Size: Up to 6 inches (15 cm) long
Diet: Dead material that has fallen to the seafloor
Predators: Fish
Life span: Unknown
Field note: A sea pig breathes through its butt. Really, it's true.

DEEP-SEA OCTOPUS

Scientific name: *Muusoctopus robustus*
Size: 15 inches (38 cm) long
Diet: Amphipods, shrimp, crabs, clams, mussels, snails, fish
Predators: Large fish, some whales
Life span: Unknown
Field note: Hundreds of deep-sea octopuses get together when they're ready to lay eggs. Each female covers her eggs with her body and waits for them to hatch.

OREGON HAIR CRAB

Scientific name: *Paralomis multispina*
Size: 3 inches (8 cm) long
Diet: Dead whales, worms, snails
Predators: Fish, octopuses, other crabs
Life span: Unknown
Field note: Oregon hair crabs have ten legs. They use eight for walking. The other two have claws for eating and defense.

BLOB SCULPIN

Scientific name: *Psychrolutes phrictus*
Size: Up to 28 inches (70 cm) long
Diet: Snails, sea slugs, shrimp, crabs, sea pigs, squid, sea cucumbers
Predators: None
Life span: Unknown
Field note: Like birds, blob sculpins lay their eggs in nests and care for them until they hatch.

ZOMBIE WORM

Scientific name: *Osedax*
Size: Females are 0.5 inch (1.3 cm) long; males are microscopic.
Diet: Dead whale bones
Predators: Crabs, amphipods
Life span: Unknown
Field note: Male zombie worms live inside the females. One female may house hundreds of itty-bitty boys.

BRITTLE STAR

Scientific name: Ophiuroid group
Size: Varies
Diet: Dead material that has fallen to the seafloor
Predators: Fish, octopuses
Life span: 5 years
Field note: A brittle star's arms can move from side to side, but not up and down.

SEA CUCUMBER

Scientific name: *Pannychia moseleyi*
Size: Up to 8 inches (20 cm) long
Diet: Dead material that has fallen to the seafloor
Predators: Fish, crabs
Life span: Up to 10 years
Field note: When an enemy attacks, this sea cucumber startles its predator by producing glowing blue bands of light.

SQUAT LOBSTER

Scientific name: *Munida quadrispina*
Size: Up to 3.5 inches (9 cm) long
Diet: Zombie worms, bacteria, dead animals
Predators: Unknown
Life span: Unknown
Field note: The squat lobster is actually a kind of crab.

PROVANNID SNAIL

Scientific name: *Provanna lomana*
Size: 0.4 inches (1 cm) long
Diet: Microbial mats
Predators: Fish, crabs
Life span: Unknown
Field note: This snail was first described in 1918 after a scientist found the shell in a museum collection.

LIMPET

Scientific name: *Cocculina craigsmithi*
Size: 1.2 inches (3 cm) long
Diet: Microbial mats
Predators: Fish, crabs
Life span: Unknown
Field note: This limpet is named after Craig Smith, the scientist who discovered that whale falls can support large communities of life for many years.

TUBEWORM

Scientific name: *Escarpia spicata*
Size: Up to 24 inches (61 cm)
Diet: Nutrients produced by bacteria living inside it
Predators: Fish, crabs
Life span: Unknown
Field note: Tubeworms are closely related to zombie worms. They are distantly related to earthworms.

CLAM

Scientific name: Vesicomyid family
Size: Varies
Diet: Nutrients produced by bacteria living inside it
Predators: Fish, crabs
Life span: Unknown
Field note: A young clam gets the bacteria living inside it from its mother.

MUSSEL

Scientific name: *Idas washingtonia*
Size: Up to 0.4 inches (1 cm) long
Diet: Nutrients produced by bacteria living inside it
Predators: Fish, crabs
Life span: Unknown
Field note: These mussels begin life as males. They turn into females when they are 0.2 inches (0.6 cm) long.

SCALE WORM

Scientific name: *Bathykurila guaymasensis*
Size: 0.3 inches (0.8 cm) long
Diet: Microbial mats
Predators: Unknown
Life span: Unknown
Field note: A scale worm has four sets of jaws.

SELECTED SOURCES

Blue Planet II: Seas of Life. Dolby digital 5.1, 420 minutes. London: BBC Earth, 2018, DVD.

Braby, Caren E., Greg W. Rouse, Shannon B. Johnson, William J. Jones, Robert C. Vrijenhoek. "Bathymetric and Temporal Variation Among *Osedax* Boneworms and Associated Megafauna on Whale-falls in Monterey Bay, California." *Deep Sea Research Part I: Oceanographic Research Papers.* October 2007, 54(10), pp. 1773–1791.

Dybas, Cheryl Lyn. "Undertakers of the Deep." *Natural History.* November 1999, 108, pp. 40–47.

Feldman, Robert A., Timothy Shank, Michael B. Black, Amy R. Baco, Craig R. Smith, and Robert C. Vrijenhoek. "Vestimentiferan on a Whale Fall." *The Biological Bulletin.* May 1998, 194(2), pp. 116–119.

"Fleshing Out the Life Histories of Dead Whales." Monterey Bay Aquarium Research Institute. Monterey Bay, CA, December 6, 2010. mbari.org/fleshing-out-the-life-histories-of-dead-whales

Fulton-Bennet, Kim. "Whale Falls—Islands of Abundance and Diversity in the Deep Sea." Monterey Bay Aquarium Research Institute. Monterey Bay, CA, December 20, 2002. mbari.org/whale-falls-islands-of-abundance-and-diversity-in-the-deep-sea

Goffredi, Shana K., Regina Wilpiszeski, Ray Lee, and Victoria J. Orphan. "Temporal Evolution of Methane Cycling and Phylogenetic Diversity of Archaea in Sediments from a Deep-sea Whale-fall in Monterey Canyon, California." *International Society for Microbial Ecology.* June 2008, 2, pp. 204–220.

Honeyborne, James, and Mark Brownlow. *Blue Planet II: A New World of Hidden Depths.* London: BBC Books, 2017.

Little, Crispin, T. S. "Life at the Bottom: The Prolific Afterlife of Whales." *Scientific American.* February 2010, pp. 78–84.

Lundsten, Lonny, Kyra L. Schlining, Kaitlin Frasier, Shannon B. Johnson, Linda A. Kuhnz, Julio B. J. Harvey, Gillian Clague, and Robert C. Vrijenhoek. "Time-series Analysis of Six Whale-fall Communities in Monterey Canyon, California, USA." *Deep Sea Research Part I: Oceanographic Research Papers.* December 2010, 57(12), pp. 1573–1584.

Milius, Susan. "Decades of Dinner: Underwater Community Begins with the Remains of a Whale." *Science News.* May 7, 2005, 167(19), pp. 298–299.

Monterey Bay Aquarium Research Institute (MBARI) Deep-Sea Guide, dsg.mbari.org/dsg/home

Smith, Craig R., and Amy R. Baco. "Ecology of Whale Falls at the Deep-Sea Floor." *Oceanography and Marine Biology: An Annual Review.* 2003, 41, pp. 311–354.

Smith, Craig R., Adrian G. Glover, Tina Treude, Nicholas D. Higgs, and Diva J. Amon. "Whale-Fall Ecosystems: Recent Insights into Ecology, Paleoecology, and Evolution." *Annual Review of Marine Science.* 2015, 7, pp. 571–596.

Treude, Tina, Craig R. Smith, Frank Wenzhöfer, Erin Carney, Angelo F. Bernardino, Angelos K. Hannides, Martin Krüger, and Antje Boetius. "Biogeochemistry of a Deep-sea Whale Fall: Sulfate Reduction, Sulfide Efflux and Methanogenesis." *Marine Ecology Progress Series.* April 30, 2009, 382, pp. 1–21.

FOR FURTHER EXPLORATION

BOOKS AND ARTICLES

Bardoe, Cheryl. "Living in the Dark: In the Deepest Parts of the Ocean, Life Springs from Surprising Places." *Muse,* February 2012, 16(2), pp. 6–8.

Collard, Sneed B. III. *The Deep-Sea Floor.* Watertown, MA: Charlesbridge, 2003.

Cusolito, Michelle. *Flying Deep: Climb Inside Deep-Sea Submersible Alvin.* Watertown, MA: Charlesbridge, 2018.

Rosenstock, Barb. *Otis and Will Discover the Deep: The Record-Setting Dive of the Bathysphere.* New York: Little, Brown, 2018.

"When a Whale Falls." *Ask,* October 2019, 18(8), pp. 24–25.

PHOTOS AND VIDEOS

"Diving on the Rosebud Whale Fall." Nautilus Live. Ocean Exploration Trust. nautiluslive.org/album/2015/08/01/diving-rosebud-whale-fall

"Images Related to the MRARI News Release Fleshing Out the Life Histories of Dead Whales." Monterey Bay Aquarium Research Institute. Monterey Bay, CA, December 6, 2010. mbari.org/images-related-to-the-mbari-news-release-fleshing-out-the-life-histories-of-dead-whales

"Observing a Natural Whale Fall." Nautilus Live. Ocean Exploration Trust. nautiluslive.org/video/2016/08/03/observing-natural-whale-fall

"Whale Fall Actively Devoured by Scavengers at Davidson Seamount." Nautilus Live. Ocean Exploration Trust. nautiluslive.org/video/2019/10/16/whale-fall-actively-devoured-scavengers-davidson-seamount

"Whale Fall at Santa Cruz Basin." Nautilus Live. Ocean Exploration Trust. nautiluslive.org/album/2017/07/21/whale-fall-santa-cruz-basin